SHORT WALKS
PEAK DISTRICT
EDALE AND THE HOPE VALLEY

by Andrew McCloy

A remote hill farm above Bretton Clough (Walk 12)

CONTENTS

Using this guide... 4
Route summary table 6
Map key 7
Introduction... 9
  Walking in Edale and the Hope Valley............................. 10
  Travel and bases... 10
  Looking after the national park.................................. 11

The walks

1.	Kinder Scout via Ringing Roger and Grindslow Knoll	13
2.	Edale: Upper Booth and Barber Booth	19
3.	Hollins Cross and Mam Tor	23
4.	Castleton and the caverns	29
5.	Castleton and Hope	35
6.	Win Hill	41
7.	Hope to Edale	47
8.	Ladybower Reservoir	53
9.	Bamford	59
10.	Stanage Edge and North Lees	65
11.	Hathersage	69
12.	Bretton Clough	73
13.	Eyam	79
14.	Higger Tor and Carl Wark	85
15.	Longshaw	91

Useful information... 95

USING THIS GUIDE

Routes in this book

In this book you will find a selection of easy or moderate walks suitable for almost everyone, including casual walkers and families with children, or for when you only have a short time to fill. The routes have been carefully chosen to allow you to explore the area and its attractions. Most routes are circular or out-and-back, although some linear walks may be included that use public transport to get back to the start. Although there may be some climbs there is no challenging terrain, but do bear in mind that conditions can sometimes be wet or muddy underfoot. A route summary table is included on page 6 to help you choose the right walk.

Clothing and footwear

You won't need any special equipment to enjoy these walks. The weather in Britain can be changeable, so choose clothing suitable for the season and wear or carry a waterproof jacket. For footwear, comfortable walking boots or trainers with a good grip are best. A small rucksack for drinks, snacks and spare clothing is useful. See www.adventuresmart.uk.

Walk descriptions

At the beginning of each walk you'll find all the information you need:

- start/finish location, with a what3words address to help you find it
- parking and transport information, estimated walking time, total distance and climb
- details of public toilets available along the route and where you can get refreshments
- a summary of the key highlights of the walk and what you might see

Timings given are the time to complete the walk at a reasonable walking pace. Allow extra time for extended stops or if walking with children.

The route is described in clear, easy-to-follow directions, with each waypoint marked on an accompanying map extract. It's a good idea to read the whole of the route instructions before setting out, so that you know what to expect.

Maps, GPX files and what3words

Extracts from the OS® 1:25,000 map accompany each route. GPX files for all the walks in this book are available to download at www.cicerone.co.uk/1258/gpx.

What3words is a free smartphone app which identifies every 3m square of the globe with a unique three-word address, e.g. ///destiny.cafe.sonic. For more information see https://what3words.com/products/what3words-app.

USING THIS GUIDE

Walking with children

Even young children can be surprisingly strong walkers, but every family is different and you may need to adapt the timings given in this book to take that into account. Make sure you go at the pace of the slowest member and choose a walk with an exciting objective in mind, such as a cave, river, waterfall or picnic spot. Many of the walks can be shortened to suit – suggestions are included at the end of the route description.

Dogs

Sheep or cattle may be found grazing on a number of these walks. Keep dogs under control at all times so that they don't scare or disturb livestock or wildlife. Cattle, particularly cows with calves, may very occasionally pose a risk to walkers with dogs. If you ever feel threatened by cattle, you should let go of your dog's lead and let it run free.

Enjoying the countryside responsibly

Enjoy the countryside and treat it with respect to protect our natural environments. Stick to footpaths and take your litter home with you. When driving, slow down on rural roads and park considerately, or better still use public transport. For more details check out www.gov.uk/countryside-code.

The Countryside Code

Respect everyone
- be considerate to those living in, working in and enjoying the countryside
- leave gates and property as you find them
- do not block access to gateways or driveways when parking
- be nice, say hello, share the space
- follow local signs and keep to marked paths unless wider access is available

Protect the environment
- take your litter home – leave no trace of your visit
- do not light fires and only have BBQs where signs say you can
- always keep dogs under control and in sight
- dog poo – bag it and bin it – any public waste bin will do
- care for nature – do not cause damage or disturbance

Enjoy the outdoors
- check your route and local conditions
- plan your adventure – know what to expect and what you can do
- enjoy your visit, have fun, make a memory

ROUTE SUMMARY TABLE

WALK NAME	START POINT	TIME	DISTANCE
1. Kinder Scout via Ringing Roger and Grindslow Knoll	Old Nags Head pub, Edale	3hr	7.2km (4.5 miles)
2. Edale: Upper Booth and Barber Booth	Edale car park	1hr 30min	6km (3.7 miles)
3. Hollins Cross and Mam Tor	Edale car park	2hr	6km (3.7 miles)
4. Castleton and the caverns	Castleton Visitor Centre	2hr 30min	8km (5 miles)
5. Castleton and Hope	Castleton Visitor Centre	2hr	6.8km (4.2 miles)
6. Win Hill	St Peter's Church, Hope	2hr 45min	7.5km (4.7 miles)
7. Hope to Edale	Hope station	3hr	10.8km (6.7 miles)
8. Ladybower Reservoir	Fairholmes Visitor Centre	2hr 45min	9.1km (5.7 miles)
9. Bamford	Heatherdene	2hr 45min	8.5km (5.3 miles)
10. Stanage Edge and North Lees	Hollin Bank car park	2hr	5.5km (3.4 miles)
11. Hathersage	Village information point, Hathersage	1hr 15min	2.8km (1.7 miles)
12. Bretton Clough	Barrel Inn, Bretton	2hr	5.5km (3.4 miles)
13. Eyam	Eyam Museum	2hr	5.5km (3.4 miles)
14. Higger Tor and Carl Wark	Upper Burbage Bridge	1hr 30min	5km (3.1 miles)
15. Longshaw	Longshaw Visitor Centre	1hr 30min	4.9km (3 miles)

ROUTE SUMMARY TABLE

HIGHLIGHTS
High-level adventure, rocky tors, hilltop views
Historic settlements, gentle valley-bottom scenery
Hilltop and ridge path, panoramic views
Caverns, castle, dramatic limestone gorge
Gentle valley route, villages and views
Ascent of mini summit, spectacular panoramic views
Linear walk through two valleys, historic routes
Picturesque waterside paths, history
Views from rocky escarpment, giant reservoir dam
Climbing crags, sweeping moorland vista
Lively village, literary and folklore connections
Peaceful valley, moors, woodland, birdlife
Village heritage, buildings and plague story
Moorland history, ancient hillfort, views
Scenic estate, easy paths, moorland views

SYMBOLS USED ON ROUTE MAPS

 Start point

 Finish point

 Start and finish at the same place

 Waypoint

~ Route line

MAPPING IS SHOWN AT A SCALE OF 1:25,000

0 KM   0.25   0.5
0 miles   0.25

DOWNLOAD THE GPX FILES FOR FREE AT
www.cicerone.co.uk/1258/gpx

Higger Tor (Walk 14; photo: Mat Robinson)

INTRODUCTION

Edale valley (Walks 1, 2, 3 and 7)

Imagine for a moment the Peak District as a giant, layered cake. The high moorland of the Dark Peak is the firm covering on the top, while at the base are the softer and delicate dales of the White Peak. Edale and the Hope Valley is the delicious filling in the middle, providing walkers with a mouth-watering treat that will satisfy every taste and appetite.

More prosaically, the Hope Valley is in effect the geological dividing line between the northern gritstone and southern limestone that have fashioned the scenery and landforms of the Peak District. The walks in this book allow you to dip into both to enjoy a variety of walking experiences, as well as to visit iconic locations like Mam Tor and Stanage Edge.

The main valley is long and straight and stretches from Hathersage in the east to Castleton at the far western end, with Edale valley swinging off to the north. Dividing the two is the so-called Great Ridge, an exhilarating switchback culminating in the towering dome of Mam Tor. The high moorland plateau of Kinder Scout and dramatic rocky escarpment of Stanage Edge provide the northern and eastern backdrops, with the Upper Derwent Valley reservoirs connected via Bamford.

This is also an important cultural landscape. From the Bronze Age hill-fort of Carl Wark to Roman roads and medieval packhorse routes across Win Hill, the walks in this book explore thousands of years of history layered upon the land. Around Hathersage and Stanage you will learn how it inspired one of our greatest novelists, and how, too, public access to the moors of Kinder Scout itself became the focus of radical campaigning; plus there are moving historical tales of heroism and sacrifice at Eyam and Ladybower. And although today the valley's economy is strongly visitor-based, traditional livelihoods like farming and quarrying are still very much alive, and deep-rooted community events, such as Hope agricultural show and Castleton's unusual garland ceremony, make this a vibrant and stimulating place to visit.

Walking in Edale and the Hope Valley

The short walks in this book are nearly all circular and generally follow good, well-signposted paths. There are energetic hill walks to spectacular viewpoints like Mam Tor and Win Hill, two of the few real 'peaks' of the Peak District, and to the elevated heather moors and rocky outcrops of Kinder Scout and Bamford Edge, where the terrain is steeper and the paths can be rougher underfoot. Lower down, the lush valley scenery around the villages of Edale and Hope provides gentler routes, plus there are easy trails along Ladybower Reservoir's attractive tree-lined shore and around the National Trust's Longshaw estate. Discover a secret wooded valley at Bretton Clough; admire climbers scaling the crags of Stanage Edge; and learn how Castleton's cavernous riches are found both above and below ground.

Travel and bases

Edale and the Hope Valley are highly accessible locations and public transport can be used to reach the start of most of the walks in this book. The Hope Valley railway line provides an easy and direct route from Manchester and Sheffield, with regular services to stations at Edale, Hope, Bamford, Hathersage and Grindleford; and there's also a frequent daily bus service from Sheffield to Castleton. Nearly all the villages have pubs and cafes used to customers turning up with muddy boots, excitable children or

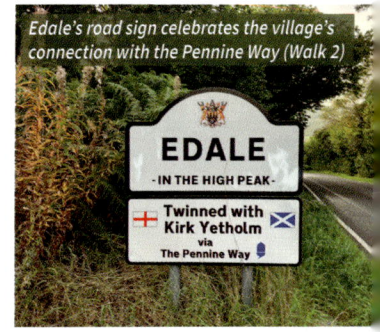
Edale's road sign celebrates the village's connection with the Pennine Way (Walk 2)

In summer the heather moors above Edale and the Hope Valley turn purple

panting dogs (and often all three at once). There are also outdoor clothing and equipment stores at Hathersage, which is handy in case you've forgotten to bring your favourite sunhat.

Most of the villages offer B&B or self-catering accommodation, with Hope providing a handy central base from which to explore. Around Castleton and Edale there are plenty of small touring caravan and campsites, as well as popular YHA hostels.

Looking after the national park

The Peak District National Park was the first to be established in Britain in 1951, but long before then it was the focus of a sometimes heated campaign for greater public access, especially to the hills and moors of the Dark Peak (see Walk 1). The national park remains very popular and some locations can get busy at peak times; however, you don't have to venture far down the path to enjoy peace and quiet and appreciate why this place is so special.

Indeed, exploring on foot is not just one of the most rewarding ways to discover the Peak District, it's also the most sustainable. The national park is a precious but fragile environment, where there's a delicate balance between recreation, conservation and the day-to-day life of local communities, so enjoy this glorious landscape – but tread lightly and be respectful.

Make sure to call into the National Park Visitor Centre in Castleton to learn more and get help with your visit; and to put something back please support the work of the Peak District National Park Foundation, a charity set up to raise funds to care for the national park (www.peakdistrictfoundation.org.uk).

The stepped path up Ringing Roger

WALK 1
Kinder Scout via Ringing Roger and Grindslow Knoll

Time 3hr
Distance 7.2km (4.5 miles)
Climb 380m

Enjoy sensational views on this energetic and adventurous walk around Edale's high skyline

Start/finish	Old Nags Head pub, Edale
Locate	///this.cobble.shredder
Cafes/pubs	Cafes and pubs in Edale
Transport	Buses from Buxton. Trains from Manchester and Sheffield
Parking	Edale car park (S33 7ZL, 5min from start)
Toilets	At Edale car park

Edale's narrow valley is dominated by the bulky outline of Kinder Scout, a high moorland plateau with steep sides and rocky outcrops. It's an iconic location among hillwalkers, not just for its dramatic upland scenery but also as the site of early protests over public access. This is an exciting but challenging route, with plenty of ascent, steep slopes and often rough underfoot. Undertake it in good weather and you'll be rewarded with magnificent views and a tremendous sense of elevation.

Edale church, with Kinder Scout providing the backdrop

The Old Nags Head at Edale

1 Walk up the lane to the left of the **Old Nags Head** pub. Branch right before a white gate for a narrow, wooded path that crosses the brook by a footbridge. Back out in the open, continue on a paved path for 150m until you reach a small barn on the left.

2 Veer right up the open hillside, aiming to the left of **Heardman's Plantation**. Beyond a gate follow the rising path up a series of long switchbacks past **The Nab**. Ignore paths off to the right and after 1.3km you reach a path junction with the crags of **Ringing Roger** directly above.

Heardman's plantation is named after Fred Heardman, the legendary landlord of the Old Nags Head in the 1950s, who supported the newly created national park by effectively turning his pub into the first information centre and wardens' base.

3 Go up the stepped route ahead for a path just below and left of the summit (or take the left-hand choice for a lower and easier path around Ringing Roger which joins the other path further on). From Ringing Roger continue uphill until you reach the very top and the main route around the southern edge of Kinder Scout. As well as Ringing Roger, other evocatively named rock formations on Kinder Scout include Madwoman's Stones, Wool Packs, Noe Stool and Seal Stones.

WALK 1 – KINDER SCOUT VIA RINGING ROGER AND GRINDSLOW KNOLL

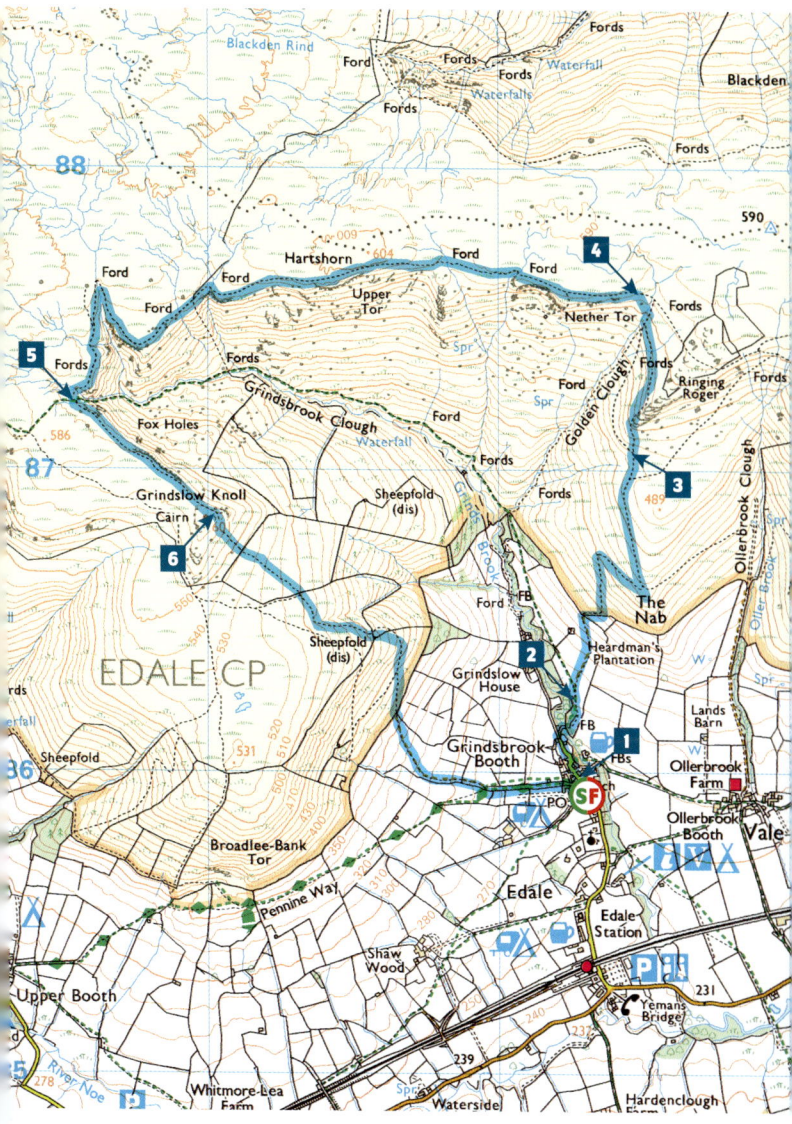

4 Turn left and follow the well-walked route along the high and in places steep rim of the hilltop. Sometimes it's a paved path, but elsewhere it simply threads its way through the rocks and heather. After 2.5km you reach a large cairn by a junction of routes at the top of **Grindsbrook Clough**.

> Kinder Scout summit plateau was once notorious for its bare and eroded peat, damaged by centuries of pollution, fires and overgrazing, but since 2010 pioneering restoration work has helped the moorland recover, with benefits for both nature and climate (www.moorsforthefuture.org.uk).

> ⓘ *The Peak District National Park has around 500km² (193 sq miles) of designated Open Access Land where the public has a right to roam freely on foot.*

5 Maintaining your height, now swing left (south-east) on a clear path, making sure not to drop down into Grindsbrook Clough. Keep this deep valley below on your left and follow a gently rising route across rough grass and heather to reach the prominent top of **Grindslow Knoll**.

6 Beyond the summit continue on the wide path, a little rough in places, that makes a long and steady descent

Edale from Kinder Scout

The path on Kinder Scout is paved in places to prevent erosion

all the way back down the open hillside to **Edale**, in sight below. Follow waymarks through the final field for a shady sunken path that emerges by the **Old Nags Head** pub.

Kinder Scout and the campaign for public access

At 636m Kinder Scout is the highest point in Derbyshire and the Peak District National Park. A century ago it was largely out of bounds to the public, privately owned and managed as an exclusive grouse-shooting estate. In 1932 a group of young ramblers staged a mass trespass in protest; despite a harsh response from the authorities, with some even sent to prison, it generated considerable publicity and popular support for the wider access campaign. When the Peak District National Park was established 20 years later new access agreements to Kinder Scout were soon reached; and in 1982 the estate was acquired by the National Trust and public access guaranteed forever.

Paved path near Grindsbrook Booth

WALK 2
Edale: Upper Booth and Barber Booth

Start/finish	*Edale car park*
Locate	*///bagpipes.shook.petition*
Cafes/pubs	*Cafes and pubs in Edale*
Transport	*Buses from Buxton. Trains from Manchester and Sheffield*
Parking	*Edale car park (S33 7ZL)*
Toilets	*At Edale car park*

Time 1hr 30min
Distance 6km (3.7 miles)
Climb 125m

A gentle and low-level wander around the valley connecting several of Edale's historic booths

Edale is made up of five separate hamlets that began as temporary shelters, known as booths, which were used by herdsmen to manage livestock grazing in the valley. This straightforward walk links three of them, crossing gentle slopes and field paths which in one place may be a little muddy after rain. The first stretch is from Grindsbrook Booth to Upper Booth and follows the easy opening stage of the famous Pennine Way – the long-distance trail gets much harder further on!

The head of the Edale valley

The path from Grindsbrook Booth to Upper Booth

1 Go down the steps by the toilet block on the edge of the car park. Turn right and walk up the road under the railway bridge all the way until you reach Edale School by the **Old Nags Head** pub.

2 Turn left, past a plaque marking the official start of the **Pennine Way** (complete with spelling mistake!) and follow a shaded sunken path.

> When it opened in 1965, the Pennine Way was Britain's first official long-distance path and it soon became synonymous with challenge, adventure and (for some) suffering. High level, often spectacular but also remote, the 429km trail runs from Edale all the way to Scotland.

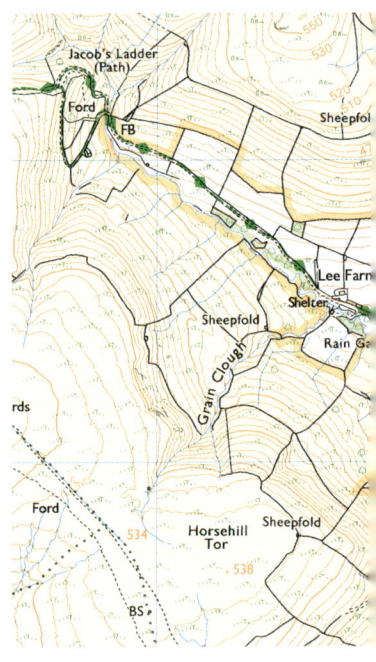

WALK 2 – EDALE: UPPER BOOTH AND BARBER BOOTH

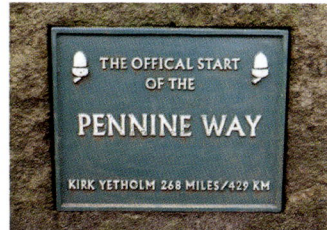

Plaque marking the start of the Pennine Way at Edale

At a junction at the top, still on the Pennine Way, branch left for a path up and across undulating valley fields below **Broadlee-Bank Tor**. After just over 2km drop down to the buildings of **Upper Booth**.

3 Just before you round the corner into the farmyard, go left through a gate. The route crosses a series of rough fields and joins a vehicle track. Follow this over a railway bridge into **Barber Booth**. Go past **Whitmore Lea Farm** and the Methodist Chapel to a junction at the end. To the west the Manchester railway line disappears into Cowburn Tunnel, which at 267m is the deepest railway tunnel in England.

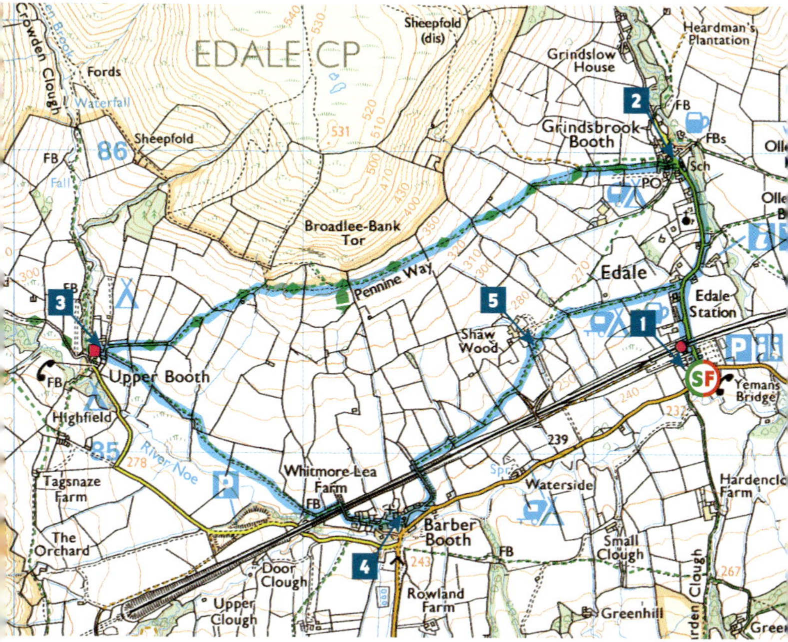

Barber Booth Methodist Chapel

4 Ignoring the main road in sight to the right, turn left and then in 100m branch left again on a path that goes back over the railway. Swing right and walk across fields, ignoring a right turn to Edale station, until you reach the drive to **Shaw Wood Farm**.

5 Go across the farm drive, up steps and through a gate, then half right at the signpost to cross the field. Follow the left side of the next field all the way back to **Edale** village. At the road turn right to return to the start.

Each September Edale hosts the Great Kinder Barrel Race, which sees teams of eight fell runners carrying a full beer barrel up and back down Kinder Scout to raise money for local village schools. It's great fun for onlookers, probably less so for competitors!

+ To lengthen

At Upper Booth (Waypoint 3) continue through the farm and turn right along the lane and then a track as far as the foot of Jacob's Ladder and the dramatic head of the valley, a there-and-back round trip along the Pennine Way of 3.5km (around 1hr).

Edale and its booths

Edale is made up of Grindsbrook Booth, Upper Booth and Barber Booth (all linked on this walk), plus Ollerbrook Booth and Nether Booth. The term 'booth' was first used in medieval times and reflects the valley's long association with sheep and cattle rearing. As the booths developed into individual farming communities, Grindsbrook, the central of the five, became the focal point and is where the pubs, school, church and station are all located. Today they're more usually and collectively known as Edale, which itself is a local term first recorded in the Domesday Book and means 'an island of ground between streams'.

WALK 3
Hollins Cross and Mam Tor

Start/finish	*Edale car park*
Locate	*///bagpipes.shook.petition*
Cafes/pubs	*Cafes and pubs in Edale*
Transport	*Buses from Buxton. Trains from Manchester and Sheffield*
Parking	*Edale car park (S33 7ZL)*
Toilets	*At Edale car park*

Time 2hr
Distance 6km (3.7 miles)
Climb 280m

A long but steady walk to the top of an iconic Peak District hill for spectacular all-round views

The dramatic Great Ridge forms Edale's southern skyline and this walk climbs gradually up to the crest and then along to the broad summit of Mam Tor. Despite the ascent, the paths are not overly steep and on the very top are wide and mostly paved. This means you can relax and enjoy the sensational views which take in the whole length of the Hope Valley.

Edale valley from the path to Hollins Cross

The Great Ridge provides exhilarating walking

1 Go down the steps by the toilet block on the edge of the car park. Turn left, then right at the road junction. After 100m turn left and walk up the surfaced drive (a public bridleway) to **Hardenclough Farm**. Continue along the lane for a further 500m, crossing a stream in a wooded dell and ignoring paths off, until you reach the very top near a private property called **Greenlands**.

> As you make your way up the hillside keep an eye on the skies above. Mam Tor is a popular location for hang-gliders and paragliders, who take off from near the summit to ride the thermals.

2 Go left through a gate, then left again through a second gate, for a path that climbs steadily up and across the open hillside to **Hollins Cross**. Hollins Cross is the mid point in the Great Ridge, a glorious high-level path that runs for 4km from Mam Tor to Lose Hill.

> At Hollins Cross you are standing at a geological divide. To the north, across the Edale valley, is the high and rigid gritstone moorland of Kinder Scout and the Dark Peak, while southwards beyond Castleton is the lower, angular and lighter limestone of the White Peak.

3 Turn right at the top for the broad ridge path that leads all the way to the summit of **Mam Tor** in view ahead.

WALK 3 – HOLLINS CROSS AND MAM TOR

Like other well used local paths, including some of the Pennine Way on Kinder Scout, the route over Mam Tor has been paved with old flagstones (reclaimed from disused local mills) to minimise human impact on this easily eroded environment.

Mam Tor's paved summit

SHORT WALKS PEAK DISTRICT

4 Continue past the summit cairn and down the stepped path beyond until you reach the road at Mam Nick. Turn right and walk carefully along the side of the road for 150m, then go right again to reach a path junction.

5 Take the lower (left) of two sign-posted routes, which drops directly down the hillside towards Edale. Join the outward route at Waypoint 2 and follow this all the way back to **Edale** and the start.

Walkers leaving Mam Tor for the Great Ridge path

Snaking road into Edale below Mam Tor

WALK 3 – HOLLINS CROSS AND MAM TOR

> ### ✚ To lengthen
> Turn left at Waypoint 3 for an undulating and panoramic walk along the Great Ridge to the summit of Lose Hill, a return distance of 4km (at least 1hr) and involving an extra 100m of ascent.

The Shivering Mountain

Subsidence on the abandoned A625 below Mam Tor

People have gazed out from the broad, domed top of Mam Tor ever since Bronze Age settlers built a hillfort on the summit. Their defensive earthwork rings are still visible, but on the side facing Castleton and the Hope Valley a large chunk of the lower hillside has literally slipped away due to the inherent instability of the overlying shale, mudstone and sandstone. The so-called Shivering Mountain is also responsible for the main road at its foot being permanently closed to traffic in the 1970s, after successive landslips rendered it unusable and uneconomic to repair. The former A625 is still visible far below as you make your way up to the summit from Hollins Cross.

The rocky descent of Cave Dale with Peveril Castle above

WALK 4
Castleton and the caverns

Start/finish	*Castleton Visitor Centre, Buxton Road*
Locate	*///imprinted.grace.pinks*
Cafes/pubs	*Wide choice in Castleton*
Transport	*Buses from Sheffield, Bakewell and Buxton*
Parking	*Castleton car park, Cross Street (S33 8WH)*
Toilets	*At Castleton car park*

Time 2hr 30min
Distance 8km (5 miles)
Climb 270m

A scenic and energetic circuit of Castleton taking in a castle, caverns and limestone gorge

The popular village of Castleton at the head of the Hope Valley is surrounded by dramatic limestone scenery, including towering cliffs and plunging slopes, as well as the looming presence of Mam Tor. This varied and adventurous route heads up and out of the main valley past the entrances to Castleton's famous show caverns, before crossing the open plateau above and returning on a rocky path through a deep gorge below the remains of a Norman castle.

A busy junction at the head of Cave Dale

SHORT WALKS PEAK DISTRICT

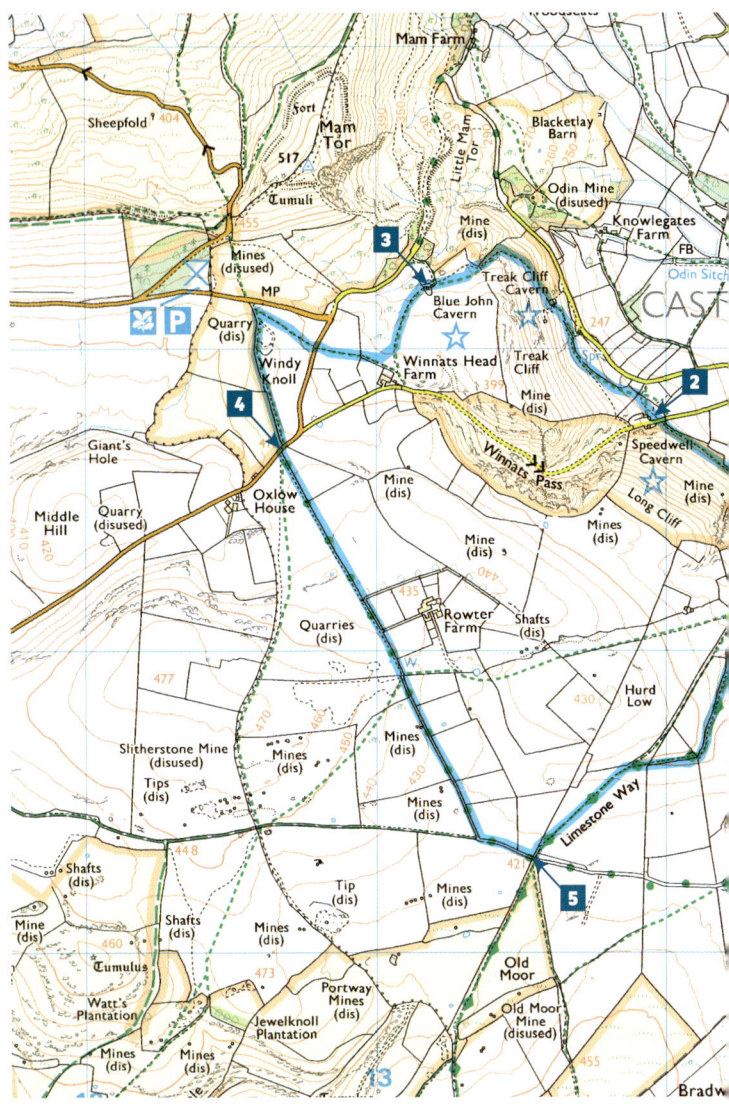

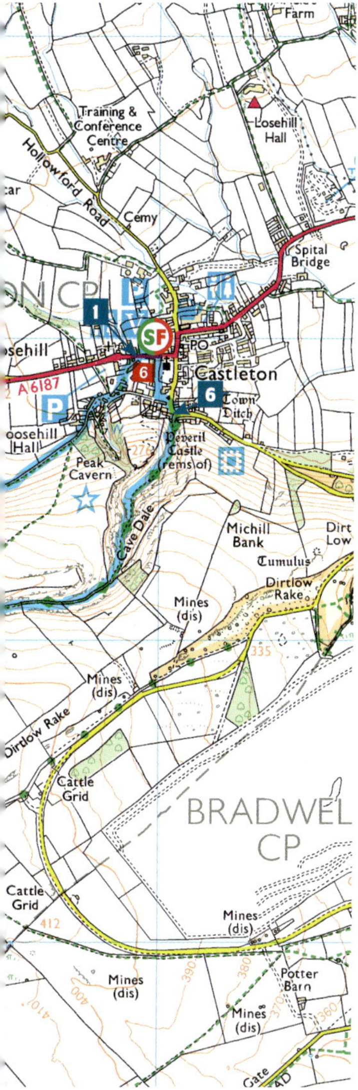

WALK 4 – CASTLETON AND THE CAVERNS

Speedwell Cavern and the entrance to Winnats Pass

1 Outside the visitor centre cross the main road at the mini roundabout, then go straight ahead between a cafe and jewellery shop for a surfaced path alongside a stream. At the end turn right into a lane called Goosehill. Follow this past the turning for **Peak Cavern** and at the far end continue along an open path beside a wall for just over 1km until you reach **Speedwell Cavern**.

> The traditional name for Peak Cavern is the rather vulgar Devil's Arse, supposedly due to the sound made by water draining from the cave, but it was changed in 1842 so not to cause offence to the visiting Queen Victoria.

2 Cross the road at the entrance to Winnats Pass for a path opposite, going along the bottom of the hillside

31

Looking down the Hope Valley from the path above Treak Cliff Cavern

> ⓘ *The Dark Peak is the setting for many of Stephen Booth's acclaimed crime novels featuring police detectives Cooper and Fry.*

and keeping left of a small wood until you reach **Treak Cliff Cavern**. Continue around the back of the building, not the paved route directly uphill. Stay on this as it climbs steadily and swings left to emerge at **Blue John Cavern**.

3 Beyond the building continue on the path up the grassy hillside. At the top swing right before **Winnats Head Farm**, cross over the road and resume the route gently uphill, with Mam Tor over to your right. At the top turn left on a hard track across **Windy Knoll** to reach a road. Excavations in a shallow cave on Windy Knoll have revealed the prehistoric remains of bison, reindeer, bear and wolves.

4 Cross over the road and walk along the surfaced farm drive opposite. Stay on this for 1.5km, past the entrance to **Rowter Farm**. Ignore turnings off and at the very far end swing left to reach a junction.

5 Turn left, signposted Castleton, then almost immediately take a right fork for a grassy path down to another

> ⓘ *Scenes for the recent* Game of Thrones *prequel series,* House of the Dragon, *were shot on location in Cave Dale near Castleton.*

WALK 4 – CASTLETON AND THE CAVERNS

path junction. Go half right for a route all the way down the full length of **Cave Dale** (around 2km) that develops into a dramatic gorge and becomes very rocky underfoot. With **Peveril Castle** above, go through the gap in the cliffs to reach the road into **Castleton**.

Peveril Castle has towered above the village for almost 1000 years and was one of the earliest Norman fortresses built in England. Now in the care of English Heritage, it's open daily and the spectacular views from the top are worth the climb.

6 Turn left and walk down the road through the village, keeping left at the war memorial and right before Castleton Hall. At the end turn left by the Castle pub to return to the visitor centre. **As you walk through Castleton pause to inspect the beautiful pieces of Blue John jewellery on sale in the shops.**

Castleton's caverns and Blue John

There are four publicly accessible show caverns or caves at Castleton and if you've enjoyed exploring above ground you should certainly make time to see the riches below. Speedwell Cavern involves a subterranean boat trip along a flooded and illuminated mine tunnel, while Treak Cliff and Blue John are rich

Castleton's jewellery shops specialise in local Blue John

in stalactites formations and the famous Blue John stone. This rare and highly prized ornamental variety of fluorspar is only found in the Castleton area and the gemstones are used to produce attractive pieces of jewellery. Closest to the village is Peak Cavern, whose vast entrance was once used to manufacture ropes for the lead mining industry.

Peakshole Water and distant Mam Tor

WALK 5
Castleton and Hope

Start/finish	*Castleton Visitor Centre, Buxton Road*
Locate	*///imprinted.grace.pinks*
Cafes/pubs	*Wide choice in in Castleton*
Transport	*Buses from Sheffield, Bakewell and Buxton*
Parking	*Castleton car park, Cross Street (S33 8WH)*
Toilets	*At Castleton car park and Hope car park*

Time 2hr
Distance 6.8km (4.2 miles)
Climb 45m

This easy and scenic route sticks to low-level paths and links the Hope Valley's two main villages

Hope Valley may be encircled by hills, but the wide valley floor provides easy walking and this low-level route sticks to gentle paths. The village of Hope, with its cafes and pubs, is a useful halfway point, and as well as ever-changing views there's plenty to learn along the way about the economic and social life of the valley's communities.

Castleton village with Peveril Castle on the skyline

SHORT WALKS PEAK DISTRICT

1 Outside the visitor centre cross the main road at the mini roundabout and turn left. Walk along the main street all the way through the village centre. Just before the final houses at the very far end turn right onto a walled lane, signposted Hope. Recent excavations in the fields over to your left, near Spital Bridge, have unearthed remains of a medieval hospital.

2 The lane becomes a path beside **Peakshole Water**. Follow this route for 2km over fields and across the railway branch line to the cement works, until you come to a lane.

Hope Cement Works may seem an incongruous sight, but it pre-dates the founding of the national park by two decades and remains an important local employer.

Hope village with the cement works beyond

However, its continuing landscape impact and CO_2 emissions, as well as its ageing infrastructure, makes its long-term future questionable.

3 Turn left and walk into the centre of **Hope**. On your left is the former Hope Pinfold, a walled pound where stray animals were kept and returned on payment of a fine. At the junction by the church cross over for the road to Edale next to the Old Hall Hotel. Walk along this road for 400m and look out for a footpath on the left between houses, almost opposite Bowden Lane.

4 Take this footpath and when you reach a path junction turn right onto the path signposted **Lose Hill**. Stay on this across fields and over the railway

Losehill Hall is now home to Castleton Youth Hostel

footbridge. Go past a house and continue straight on, gently uphill, in the direction of Lose Hill for 400m to a path junction.

Each August Bank Holiday Monday the fields below you host the popular Hope Show. This large and traditional agricultural show has everything from livestock judging and show jumping to tractor rallies, crafts and horticulture (www.hopeshow.co.uk).

5 At the path junction take the waymarked route on the left in front of a gate, now heading up the valley on a direct route across fields. Go left and almost immediately right to pass in front of **Spring House Farm** on a track, joining the drive from Fields Farm to reach the back of Castleton Youth Hostel at **Losehill Hall**.

The Victorian gothic mansion of Losehill Hall is now one of YHA's most popular youth hostels and is

> ⓘ *The deepest known natural underground shaft in Britain, named Titan, is found below Castleton and has a vertical drop of 141.5m.*

WALK 5 – CASTLETON AND HOPE

open all year round. For a different overnight experience stay in one of their landpods or bell tents situated in the extensive grounds.

6 Stay on the track past the hostel car park and at the bend go straight on. Follow the path across fields and join a drive to reach **Hollowford Road**.

7 Turn left and walk down the lane into **Castleton**. Turn right opposite Mill Lane to cut through to the visitor centre.

Castleton's garland ceremony

Every year on or around 29 May Castleton celebrates Garland Day. The Garland King, on horseback and wearing an elaborate floral garland, leads a lively procession around the village (via its six pubs, of course). There's much singing and dancing, assisted by the village band, and it concludes with the garland being hoisted to the top of the church tower. The tradition is believed to have originated with the restoration of the monarchy in 1660, although some say it can be traced back to earlier pagan festivals. There's more on this unusual ceremony, including past costumes worn by the Garland King, in Castleton Historical Society's excellent museum within Castleton Visitor Centre (open daily, free admission).

Castleton garland ceremony

St Peter's Church at Hope

WALK 6
Win Hill

Start/finish	*St Peter's Church, Hope*
Locate	*///deeply.fishnet.labels*
Cafes/pubs	*Wide choice in Hope village*
Transport	*Buses from Sheffield, Bakewell and Buxton. Trains from Manchester and Sheffield (station 10min from start)*
Parking	*Hope car park, Castleton Road (S33 6RD)*
Toilets	*At Hope car park*

Time 2hr 45min
Distance 7.5km (4.7 miles)
Climb 285m

Enjoy a spectacular hilltop panorama on this energetic ascent of a shapely Peak District summit

Sitting high on the northern edge of Hope Valley, Win Hill's cone-shaped top is one of the few to live up to the Peak District's name. To reach it there's a long but steady ascent across open slopes, with a few rougher paths and steep grassy sections on the way back down. However, the magnificent 360-degree views from the summit are certainly worth the effort, taking in much of the Dark Peak moorland and Upper Derwent reservoirs.

Looking west from Win Hill summit towards Lose Hill

SHORT WALKS PEAK DISTRICT

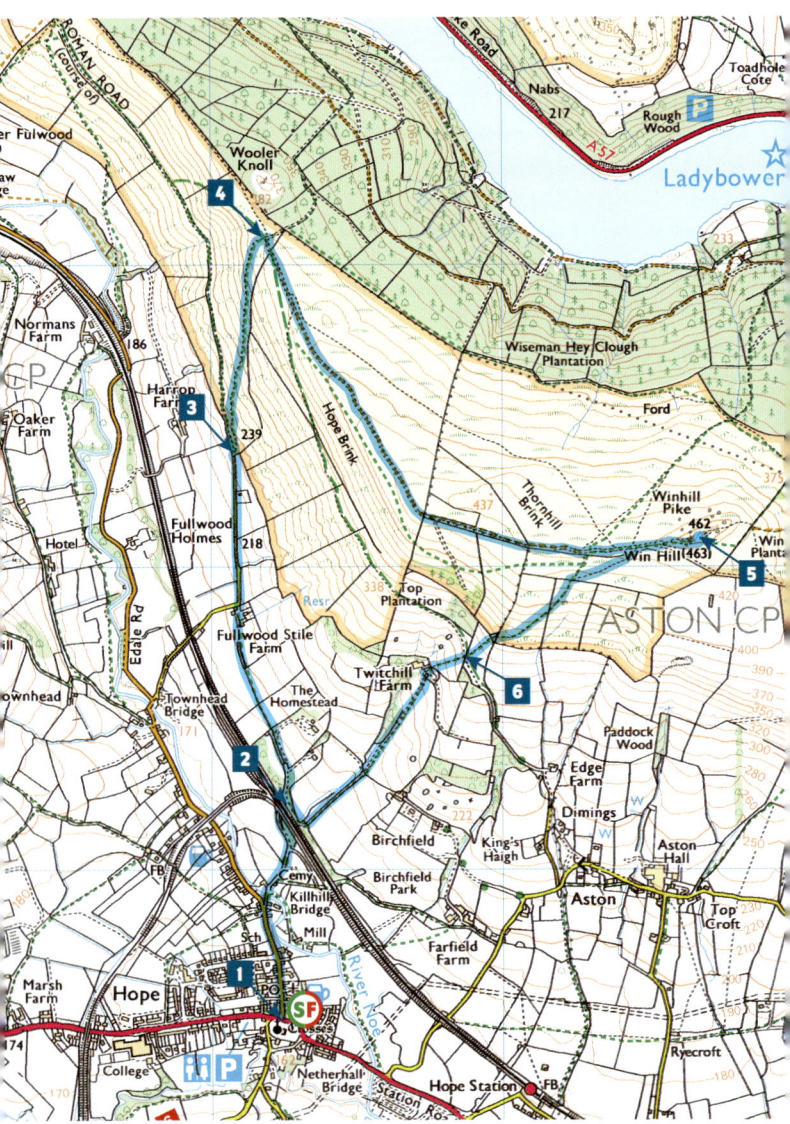

42

Old Hall Hotel near the start of the walk opposite Hope church

1 At the road junction by the church and Old Hall Hotel, walk along Edale Road for 400m and turn right onto Bowden Lane. Stay on this lane over the river and then go under the railway to reach a junction. The nearby clamour is likely to be from Earles Sidings, where heavily laden freight trains from Hope Cement Works wait to join the main line.

St Peter's Church at Hope dates from the early 14th century and has two historic ancient crosses in the churchyard. Above the main entrance, look up at the very animated stone gargoyles leering down from the top of the outer walls.

2 Turn left and keep left again, down a drive. Take the footpath that goes to the right of Coach House then out across fields. Go past **Fullwood Stile Farm** to join a lane at a bend and then go straight on until eventually you reach a gate.

ⓘ The Dark Peak moors are home to Britain's only population of mountain hares outside Scotland, notable for their coats which turn white in winter.

3 Beyond the gate take the right (upper) of two routes that slants steadily up and across the open hillside for 750m. At the very top near **Wooler Knoll** it reaches a broad track running the length of the open ridge.

4 Turn sharply right and follow the main path along the top of **Hope Brink**. In the valley far below to your left is Ladybower Reservoir, with the A57 Snake Pass winding its way across the moors to Glossop. After 2km you will reach the summit of **Win Hill**.

The angular 463m summit of Win Hill may look a little daunting from the valley floor below, but in fact the rocky pinnacle is easily and safely accessible on foot and almost flat on the very top.

5 From the summit retrace your steps along the ridge-top path for 200m, then turn left through a gate by a footpath sign. Follow this route down the hillside, aiming for Hope village in sight far below. Go through a kissing gate and straight ahead down the grassy hillside to another gate.

6 Go through the gate and continue down the steep grassy slope to reach **Twitchill Farm** immediately below. Join the farm drive and follow this all the way down to reach the railway bridge at Waypoint 2. Rejoin your outward route to return to **Hope**.

Walkers on the Win Hill ridge

Win Hill summit overlooking Ladybower Reservoir and the Dark Peak moors

+ To lengthen

At Waypoint 3 take the left (lower) route for a much gentler but longer ascent, turning sharp right at the very top to walk alongside woodland and rejoin the main route to Win Hill. This adds an extra 3km (up to 1hr).

Win some, lose some

Across the valley from Win Hill sits its counterpart Lose Hill and perhaps inevitably there has been speculation about the origin of their names. The most imaginative suggestion is that they derive from a 7th-century battle that saw Edwin of Northumbria's army, camped on what is now Win Hill, defeat a force from Wessex based on Lose Hill. Sadly there's no historical evidence to support this, and the more mundane explanation is that it comes from *wythinehull*, meaning 'withy hill' or 'willow hill', and indeed willow still grows in plantations on the hillside.

Departing Hope Station for Edale, with Lose Hill in the distance

WALK 7
Hope to Edale

Start	Hope station
Finish	Edale station
Locate	///scornful.reveal.growl
Cafes/pubs	Wide choice in Hope and Edale
Transport	Trains from Manchester and Sheffield. Buses to Hope from Sheffield, Bakewell and Buxton, buses from Edale to Buxton
Parking	Station Road, Hope (S33 6RD)
Toilets	In Hope and Edale villages

Time 3hr
Distance 10.8km (6.7 miles)
Climb 315m

A long but scenic linear walk linking the Hope and Edale valleys in the footsteps of earlier travellers

This linear walk is along a mostly elevated route with striking views throughout, linking the open and populated landscape of the Hope Valley with the more intimate scenery of Edale. But it's also about the journey itself, since these paths have been used by the Romans, packhorse traders and many other travellers over the centuries. Although it's quite long, the route is not complicated or overly difficult, plus there's a quick and easy start/finish connection by train.

Mam Tor and Hope Valley from the path below Win Hill

SHORT WALKS PEAK DISTRICT

1 Cross the footbridge at **Hope station** to the Sheffield-bound side and go right, along a footpath. This turns left and heads directly uphill across fields beside a ditch. Ignore all paths off left and right until you reach the lane at **Aston** at the very top.

> The Hope Valley railway line links Manchester and Sheffield and with frequent daily services stopping at Edale, Hope, Bamford, Grindleford and Hathersage. It's a great way to enjoy car-free walking in the Peak District.

2 Go left and immediately right for the lane uphill to **Edge Farm**, then swing left on a path to reach an open grassy area. Stay on the lower path and go through a gate on the left at the bottom of the slope.

3 Resume the same direction across the hillside, not down to the farm, walking below a small plantation and out along the clear track ahead to reach open country. Follow the track steadily up **Hope Brink** to the very top. This route was once used by the Romans to connect their fort of Melandra, near Glossop, with Navio at nearby Brough in the Hope Valley.

4 Continue ahead along the wide ridge past **Wooler Knoll**, either on the track beside the plantation or across the open but walked slope to the left

> ⓘ *Packhorse teams staying at the Cheshire Cheese inn at Hope sometimes paid for their lodgings with the goods they carried – including cheese.*

Hope Cross

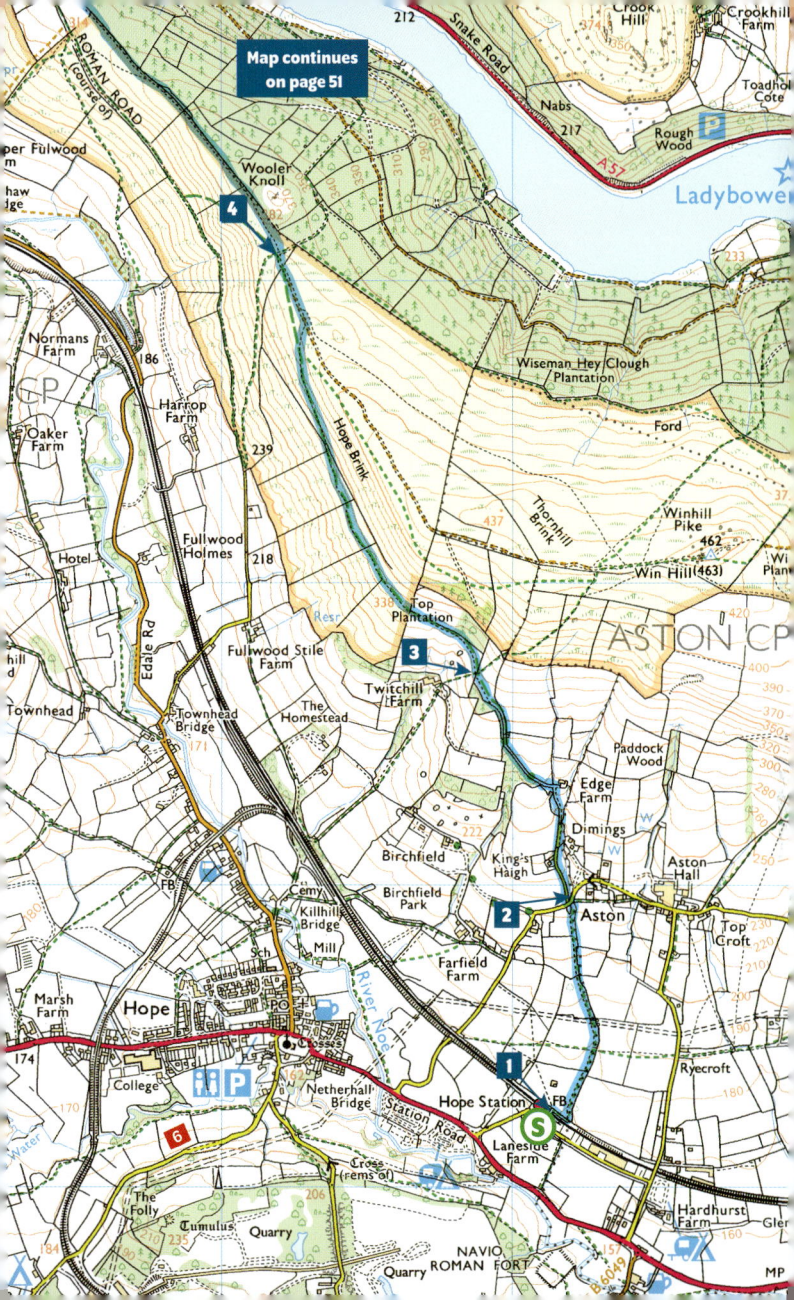

Jaggers Clough, a former packhorse route

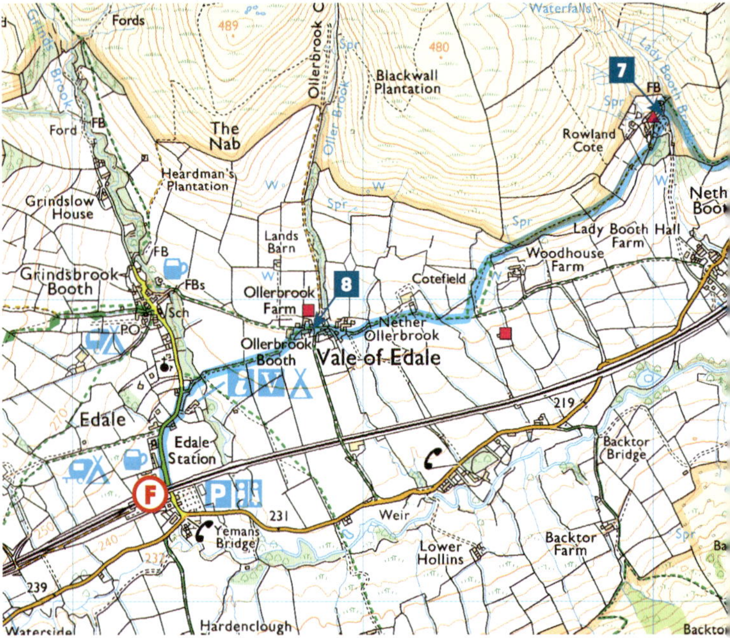

WALK 7 – HOPE TO EDALE

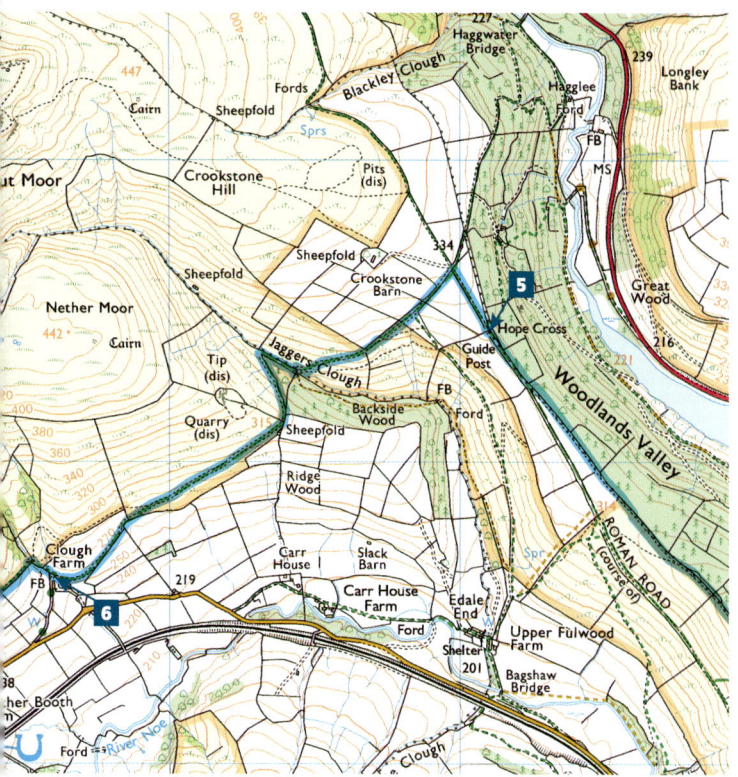

(strictly speaking the actual course of the former Roman road). Stay on this track for 2km until you reach **Hope Cross**.

The huge carved pillar of Hope Cross probably started out as a medieval stone cross, but at some point gained an overhanging square capstone inscribed with locations (Hope, Sheffield, Glossop and Edale) so that it became a guidepost for travellers.

5 Continue up to a junction of routes and turn left, signposted Edale. Follow the wide track down to cross a stream in **Jaggers Clough**, then up and across open hillside until you reach **Clough Farm**.

Edale railway station

> ⓘ *Folk musician, singer and songwriter Bella Hardy comes from Edale and draws inspiration from the landscape for her highly acclaimed work.*

The name Jaggers Clough remembers the packhorse men known as jaggers who once led lines of up to 40 heavily laden ponies along this route, carrying materials like wool, charcoal, lead ore and salt across the Peak District.

6 Go right, up the footpath beside the stream, then left to resume the route across the low hillside to Edale Youth Hostel at **Rowland Cote**.

7 Walk past the front of the building and take the path at the far end of the car park. The route soon drops down through scrub and crosses fields to reach a wide track below. Turn right and follow what is soon a surfaced drive to **Ollerbrook Booth**.

8 Go straight on through the hamlet and just past the farmhouse of Ollerbrook Farm turn left in front of some large modern barns for a track across fields to **Edale**. Cross the stream, go up to the road and turn left for **Edale station**. The Rambler pub is on one side of the bridge and the Penny Pot Cafe the other – take your pick!

WALK 8
Ladybower Reservoir

Start/finish	*Fairholmes Visitor Centre*
Locate	*///nametag.schooling.enthused*
Cafes/pubs	*Take-away kiosk at visitor centre*
Transport	*Buses from Sheffield (Sun only)*
Parking	*Fairholmes car park (S33 0AQ)*
Toilets	*At Fairholmes Visitor Centre*

Time 2hr 45min
Distance 9.1km (5.7 miles)
Climb 135m

An easy walk around the shores of a picturesque reservoir with a hidden story

Ladybower is one of three linked reservoirs that stretch northwards from Win Hill into the heart of the Dark Peak uplands. Since their construction almost a century ago these attractive, tree-lined fingers of water have become a popular visitor attraction, but their construction changed the landscape in more ways than one. This low-level route, which is direct and easy to follow, hugs the shoreline with pleasant and changing views throughout.

Fairholmes visitor centre at the start of the walk

SHORT WALKS PEAK DISTRICT

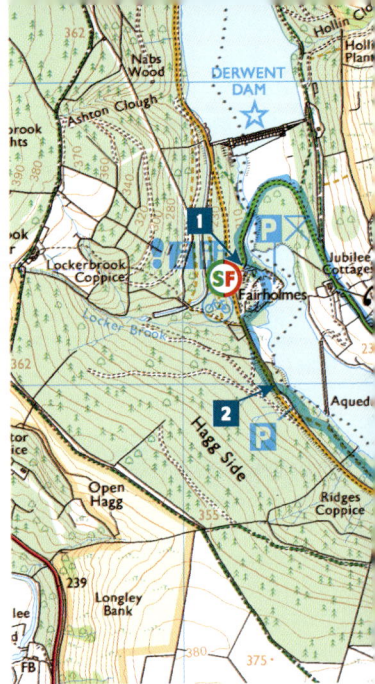

1 From the visitor centre at **Fairholmes** walk to the far side of the lower car park, with the reservoir beyond, and take the path on the right. At the far end turn left and walk along the pavement of the road as far as a parking area.

> Over 1000 people involved in building the reservoirs were housed in a temporary settlement next to Derwent Reservoir nicknamed 'Tin Town' after its corrugated iron cabins. One survives on Edale Road in Hope village, where it's now used as a hairdressers.

2 Take the signposted path on the left which leads down through trees. Follow this easy and well-walked route

Walking along Ladybower Reservoir's western shore

Ladybower viaduct with Bamford Edge in the distance

through woodland and across the open slopes above **Ladybower Reservoir**. When completely full Ladybower Reservoir can hold up to 27,870 megalitres (6.1 billion gallons) of water. After 2km you descend steps to reach a short footbridge which is part of an **aqueduct**.

3 Cross the bridge between giant water pipes and continue on the far side along the grassy slope above the shoreline until you reach the viaduct at the very far end.

Water from the three reservoirs is first pumped to Bamford treatment works for cleaning, then via gravity it flows down the 45km Derwent Valley Aqueduct to supply over half a million Severn Trent customers throughout the East Midlands every day.

4 Turn left and cross the **A57** viaduct on a wide pavement shared with cyclists. On the far side turn left up a ramped drive and at the bend go through the gate ahead. Follow this gently undulating track for 2.5km, with the reservoir now on your left, until it becomes a surfaced lane near the site of the former **Derwent** village.

Although most of Derwent village was lost forever to the new reservoir, its historic packhorse bridge was removed and rebuilt at the very head of the valley at Slippery Stones, where it continues to be used by walkers and cyclists today.

5 Stay on the lane above the reservoir. After 1.5km keep left at a fork and follow the lane down towards the foot of **Derwent Dam**. Still on the lane, swing left and beyond a bridge take the path on the left to return to the visitor centre. In World War 2 Derwent Reservoir and its dam were used by pilots of 617 Squadron ('the Dambusters') for practice flights before their bombing raids in Germany.

Derwent dam 'overtops' when the water level is exceptionally high

The lost villages of Ladybower

The creation of the three huge new reservoirs – Howden, Derwent and finally Ladybower in the 1930s–40s – was designed to cater for the rapidly expanding urban population of the East Midlands and South Yorkshire. Flooding the valley meant that two small but long-established villages, Derwent and Ashopton, together with numerous farms, had to be abandoned and their residents relocated (most to a new estate built near Bamford). There's usually no visible trace of the former villages

Traces of the former Derwent village

today, of course, but in exceptionally dry periods when the water levels drop the rather haunting foundations of the church, hall and other buildings at Derwent are revealed on the bed of Ladybower Reservoir.

The start of the walk at Heatherdene

WALK 9
Bamford

Start/finish	*Heatherdene*
Locate	*///brains.chariots.duplicate*
Cafes/pubs	*Pub with cafe in Bamford*
Transport	*Buses from Sheffield and Bakewell*
Parking	*Heatherdene car park (S33 0BY)*
Toilets	*At Heatherdene car park*

Bamford is near the intersection of the Hope and Derwent valleys, and this long and varied route begins with a climb to the top of Bamford Edge for sensational views of both. Some of the paths can be rough and be careful of sheer drops on the edge. Further down, the riverside meadows and woods offer easier walking and there's an alternative section if the River Derwent is high and the stepping stones are impassable.

Time 2hr 45min
Distance 8.5km (5.3 miles)
Climb 200m

An energetic and varied circuit of Bamford via a high rocky edge, river crossing and woodland trail

Footbridge and stepping stones over the River Derwent at Bamford Mill

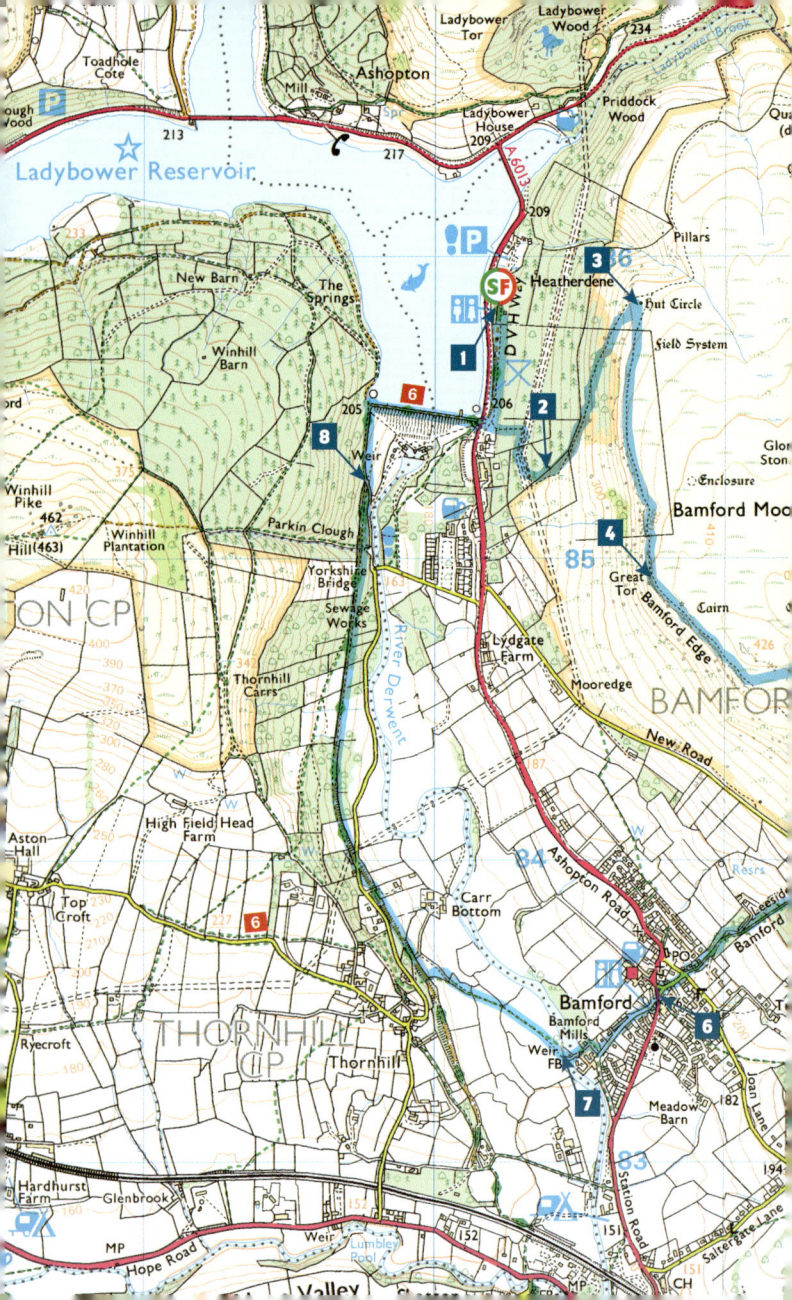

WALK 9 – BAMFORD

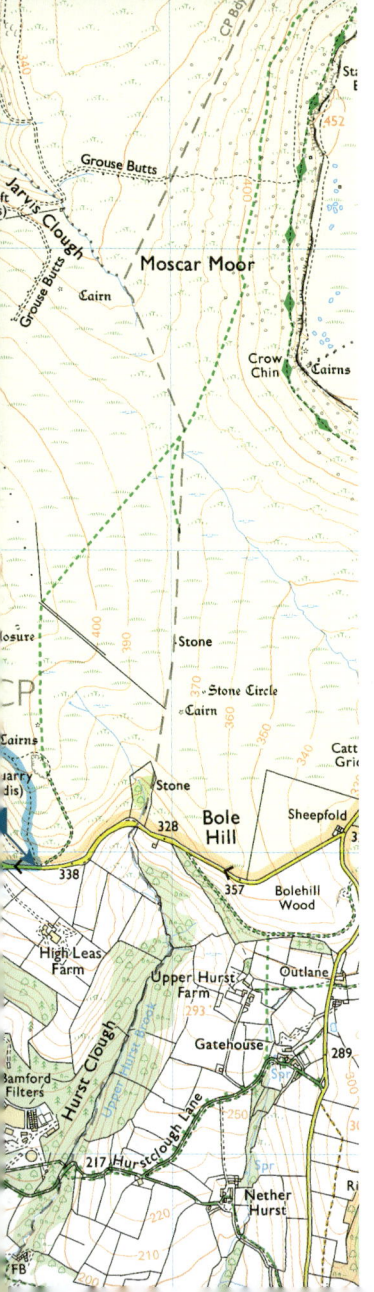

1 At the far end of the car park at **Heatherdene** follow the surfaced path past the toilets. When you draw level with the dam on your right, turn left on the waymarked 'Path to Access Land'. Go up through the trees, turn right by power lines and then uphill through more trees to reach the open hillside.

> Heatherdene is the starting point for the 89km Derwent Valley Heritage Way, a walking trail that follows the River Derwent via Chatsworth, Matlock and the Derwent Valley Mills World Heritage Site to Derby and its confluence with the River Trent.

2 Turn left and follow this well-walked route steadily uphill, at first beside the plantation then later through mixed woodland. Continue up onto **Bamford Moor** until you get to a path junction at the very top. There are numerous round cairns, stone circles and ancient field systems across Bamford Moor, many dating from the Bronze Age (around 2000BC).

3 Turn sharp right and follow the wide path to reach **Great Tor** and the rocky escarpment.

4 Continue along the top of **Bamford Edge**, ignoring a path to the right that drops straight down to the

Looking west from Bamford Edge

The Anglers Rest, Bamford

lane, and instead maintain your height until after 1.4km you descend to reach the lane at the far end.

5 Turn right, then at the top of a small plantation veer left along the surfaced track into **Bamford Clough**. Follow this long, steep route all the way downhill and into **Bamford** to reach the main road in the village centre.

For refreshments turn right to call in at the Anglers Rest in the centre of Bamford. Since 2013 the local community have owned and run this welcoming pub, which incorporates a separate cafe and post office and is open daily.

6 Go across the road and down The Hollow opposite (between stone gateposts). Follow this unmade road past houses until near the bottom it becomes surfaced. Here turn right, then left following signposts past **Bamford Mill**. Bamford Mill was built in the late 1700s as a water-powered cotton spinning mill and has now been converted to private apartments. Cross the **River Derwent** via a long footbridge preceded by stepping stones.

7 On the far bank head half right across successive gated fields, then approaching a farm go left and up to join the Thornhill Trail. Turn right and follow this for 2km, via a small car park and across a lane, until you reach the very end.

The 3.2km Thornhill Trail is part of the former railway line that was built in 1903 to transport equipment and materials used to make the giant reservoir dams, including thousands of tonnes of locally quarried stone.

8 Turn left up a surfaced lane, then go right, over the dam. What looks like two giant plugholes in the reservoir are known as bellmouth overflows and are used to regulate high water levels. Cross the main road to the memorial commemorating the dam's official opening in 1945. Go up the steps and turn left for the return path to **Heatherdene**.

– To shorten

To omit the river crossing and Thornhill Trail leave the route at Waypoint 6 and follow Ashopton Road (A6013) back to the start – the pavement is set back from the road all the way and saves 1.1km (30min).

This giant plughole acts as an overflow when the reservoir gets full

The partly paved route down Stanage Edge

WALK 10
Stanage Edge and North Lees

Start/finish	*Hollin Bank car park*
Locate	*///deaf.fluid.winter*
Cafes/pubs	*None on route*
Transport	*No public transport*
Parking	*Hollin Bank car park (S32 1BR)*
Toilets	*Near start*

Time 2hr
Distance 5.5km (3.4 miles)
Climb 220m

Climb up to a famous gritstone edge for spectacular views on this undulating valley and moorland route

The impressive 6km-long gritstone escarpment of Stanage Edge frames the eastern end of the Hope Valley and is one of the most famous climbing venues in Britain. This undulating circuit begins by exploring the attractive part-wooded hillside below, including a period house with Brontë connections, before making its way steadily up across moorland to the very top for far-reaching views. On the edge itself it can be a little uneven underfoot and be careful of sheer drops.

The Stanage escarpment stretches for over 6km

Stanage Edge from below

1 Turn left out of the car park and walk along the lane. Just after the toilets turn right for a gated path down steps signposted Hathersage and Bamford, turning right again to join a wide track downhill through a plantation. Go through another gate and take the lower of two paths across an open slope down to **North Lees Hall**.

North Lees Hall was built by Robert Eyre in the 1590s and Charlotte Brontë used it as inspiration for Thornfield, Edward Rochester's home, in her novel *Jane Eyre*. Today it's a private residence and not open to the public.

North Lees Hall

2 Continue down the drive past the Hall and turn right onto the lane at the bottom. Just past **Bronte Cottage** turn right for a path across a field. Continue through woods alongside a stream, then turn left across a footbridge and up across fields to **Green's House**. Green's House was formerly associated with nearby Green's Mill, a long-gone site of lead smelting and later a paper mill.

3 Go left into the courtyard and then right, up a walled path and out across the hillside. As you approach a small plantation at the very top, switch to the other side of the wall until you reach the road.

WALK 10 – STANAGE EDGE AND NORTH LEES

4 Turn left and walk along to the car parking area at Dennis Knoll. Turn right at the bend and follow an easy, gradual track known as **Long Causeway** for 1.5km all the way up to the top of **Stanage Edge**.

Long Causeway was originally a packhorse route linking Hope Valley to Sheffield. As use by carts and wagons increased, flat stones and cobbles known as causeys were often laid to improve the surface.

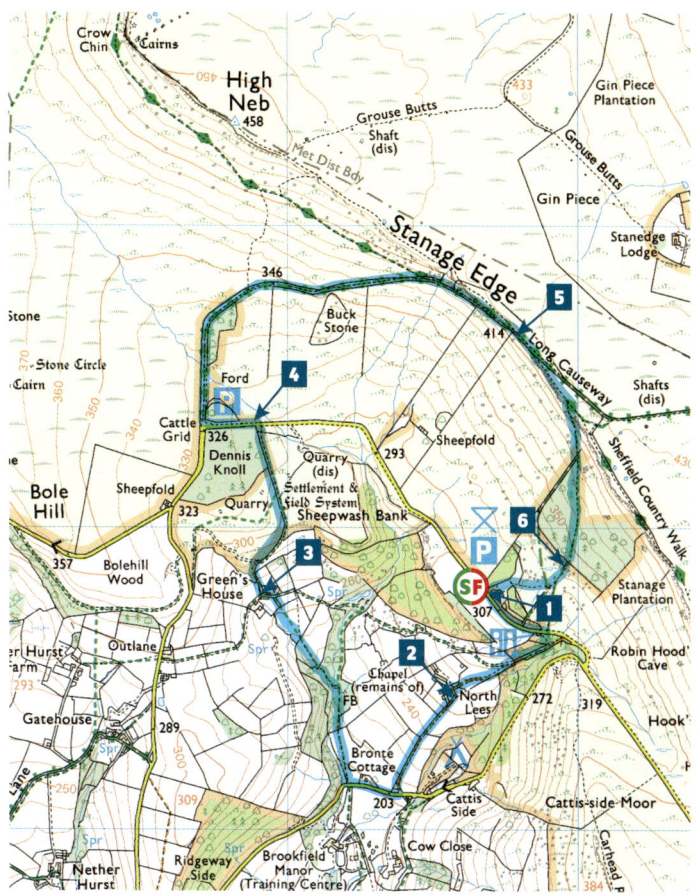

SHORT WALKS PEAK DISTRICT

> ⓘ *Three quarters of the world's heather moorland is found in the UK, with a large area in the Peak District.*

> **+ To lengthen**
>
> To explore more of Stanage Edge head left (north-west) at Waypoint 5 on the fairly level edge-top path via High Neb to Crow Chin, above Moscar Moor. This there-and-back route will take 3.5km (around 1hr) and add an extra 50m of ascent.

5 Continue straight ahead and veer right by an Access Land sign to walk along the wide, well-trodden strip just back from the top edge of the rocks. After 250m look for a roughly stepped path which winds down through a gap in the escarpment. Follow this route down across the hillside and through **Stanage Plantation**.

6 Leaving the woodland, take the right fork down to the car park or go left for the toilets.

Climbing on Stanage Edge

There are reckoned to be as many as 1900 separate climbing routes on Stanage Edge, and generations of young climbers have cut their teeth on these striking and accessible gritstone crags. The sheer variety of graded routes range from mild scrambles up to the most technically challenging ascents, with named climbs like the Unconquerables, Count's Buttress, Goliath's Groove and Eliminator. Of course, you can also enjoy Stanage with two feet firmly on the ground; and for walkers and

Climbers on Stanage Edge

climbers alike the sweeping panorama from this 450m-high vantage point, taking in the whole of Hope Valley and Kinder Scout, is simply breathtaking.

WALK 11
Hathersage

Time 1hr 15min
Distance 2.8km (1.7 miles)
Climb 115m

Start/finish	*Village information point, Main Road, Hathersage*
Locate	*///proper.refuses.flopping*
Cafes/pubs	*Wide choice in Hathersage*
Transport	*Buses from Sheffield and Bakewell. Trains from Sheffield and Manchester (station 5min from start)*
Parking	*Oddfellows Road car park, Hathersage (S32 1DU)*
Toilets	*At start*

An easy up-and-down ramble around Hathersage with intriguing literary and folklore connections

Hathersage is a large and bustling village at the eastern end of the Hope Valley whose rich heritage embraces a legendary folk hero and one of our greatest writers. This short loop involves a steady climb up the hillside above the village via lanes and paths, with one potentially muddy section, and starts at the village's central information point known as the 'Heart of Hathersage'.

Hathersage Lido has been used by the public since 1936

Looking down over Hathersage from the hillside vineyard

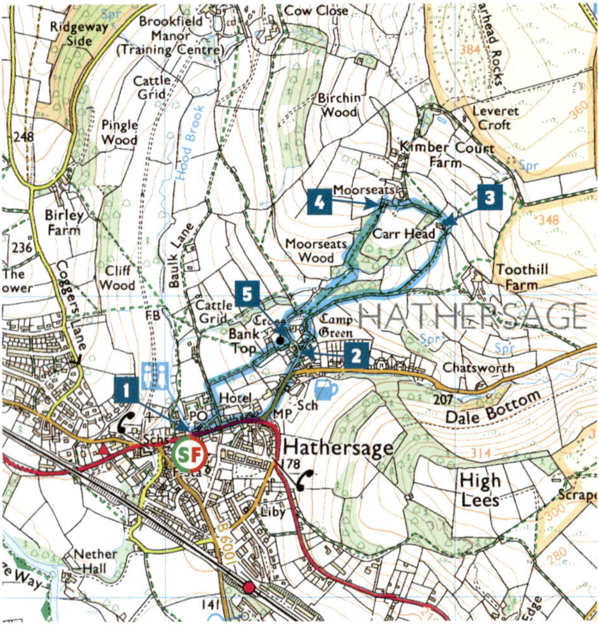

1 Walk up Main Road past the shops and cafes. Turn left into School Lane and left again into Church Bank, opposite the pub. The Scotsman's Pack is named after travelling drapers who once visited on foot from Scotland selling their homespun tweeds and woollens. Walk up the lane as far as the bend, where the church is signposted left.

2 Turn right onto a private road, which is also a public footpath. Stay on the lane past several cottages and continue climbing steadily, going left at a fork to reach **Carr Head Farm**.

You may be surprised to see the hillside below Carr Head Farm planted with vines. Hope Valley Vineyard (not open to the public) has used these high south-west facing slopes to produce still and sparkling wines for several years.

3 Continue past the buildings and on along the surfaced drive to **Moorseats Hall**. At the main entrance before the building take the narrow, gated path to the left and follow this as it drops down to enter woods.

Charlotte Brontë's visit to Hathersage in 1845 inspired her novel *Jane Eyre* (also see Walk 10). The fictitious Moor House, where Jane meets the Rivers family, was modelled on Moorseats Hall and its owner, Thomas Eyre, gave his surname to one of the most iconic literary heroines of all time.

4 Follow the obvious path gently downhill through **Moorseats Wood**, with a stream to your right. This is also known as Fairy Wood – keep your eyes peeled for unusual sights! Go through a curiously isolated doorway at the bottom and on along a path which may be muddy after rain. When you reach open ground go ahead and to the right of some buildings. At the lane turn left and then right to enter the churchyard via the main gate.

5 Walk ahead through the churchyard of **St Michaels & All Angels Church**. Little John's Grave is on

A mysterious doorway in Moorseats Wood

the left. Continue along the path past the church and downhill past the graveyard, then join a long path beside a wall. At the bottom turn left onto a wide track, then go right into Besom Lane, which brings you back out onto Main Street near to the start. Close to the start of the walk is The George, a historic coaching inn that provided inspiration for the novel *Jane Eyre*.

If you want to cool off after your walk head to Hathersage's splendid public lido on Oddfellows Road, which dates from 1936. The (heated) outdoor swimming pool is open daily, community run and has a cafe (www.hathersageswimmingpool.co.uk)

+ To lengthen

At Carr Head Farm take a waymarked footpath up the open hillside directly above, then at the top turn left along a track which drops back down to Moorseats Hall, adding a further 1.1km (30min) and 70m of ascent.

Little John's very long grave

Many believe that Robin Hood's oversized lieutenant lived in Hathersage and ended his days in a cottage near the churchyard. At that time Sherwood Forest effectively extended into the Peak District and Robin himself

Little John's Grave at Hathersage church

came from nearby Loxley, now on the edge of Sheffield. According to local folklore, Little John's bow and hat once hung inside Hathersage church and a huge thighbone was discovered when the grave was opened in the 1780s. The 3.9m-long grave is certainly an unusual sight, but distinguishing myth from reality is no easy matter.

WALK 12
Bretton Clough

Start/finish	*Barrel Inn, Bretton*
Locate	*///jets.zoos.producers*
Cafes/pubs	*Pub at Bretton*
Transport	*No public transport*
Parking	*Roadside near Barrel Inn*
Toilets	*No public toilets on route*

Time 2hr
Distance 5.5km (3.4 miles)
Climb 200m

Discover a secluded and wildlife-rich backwater on this undulating moorland and valley route

A clough is a local term for a small steep-sided valley, and this unspoilt gem, only accessible on foot, is tucked away in a fold between Eyam and Abney moors. The walk starts at the remote upland hamlet of Bretton and the undulating route, which combines open moorland and lush valley-bottom woodland, can be a little rough underfoot in places with some high stiles. However, the reward is an off-the-beaten-track journey through an undisturbed landscape full of birdlife.

The view looking south from the Barrel Inn

1 Walk down the narrow lane beside the **Barrel Inn** away from the escarpment edge to **Nether Bretton**. Follow the lane as it bends sharply right by some buildings. Continue for a further 600m, on what is now an unmade track, past a turning on the left until you reach a crossroads.

2 Turn left, over a stile beside a gate, and follow the vehicle track. When this bends right to **Stanage House** continue straight ahead. Follow the path around the right-hand edge of **Gotherage Plantation** and out onto the open hillside. Keep close to the wall on your left to reach a path junction by a signpost.

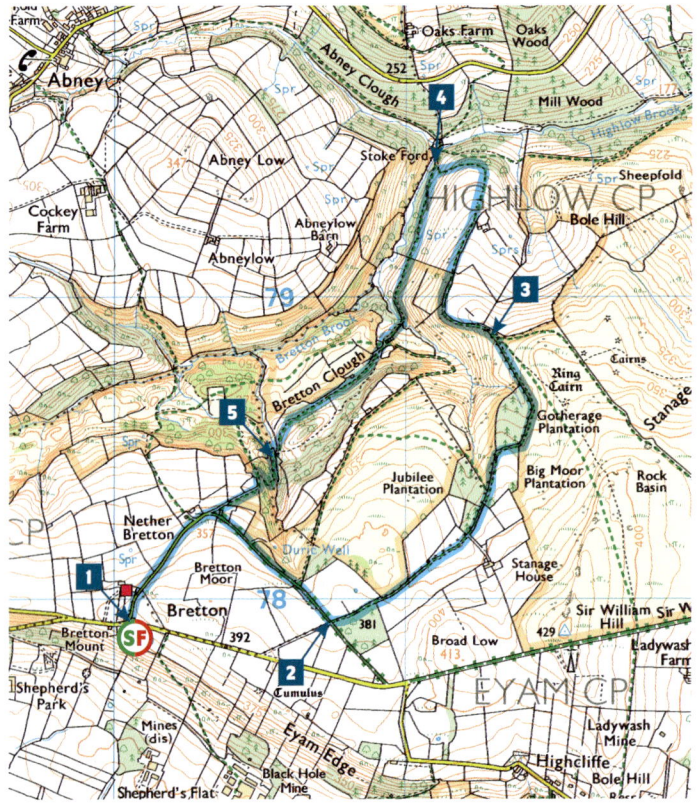

Bretton Clough – an unspoilt gem

Look out for meadow pipits and wheatears on the open moorland, with skylarks singing high above. In the sheltered scrub and woodland further down you may spot redstarts and warblers or hear the drumming of woodpeckers and the squawking of jays.

3 Continue straight on, over a wall stile by a gate, for a route along the top edge of the valley. This route was once a packhorse trail between Bradwell and Eyam. Follow it as it winds steadily downhill to a path junction almost at the bottom near **Stoke Ford**.

4 Turn left and walk along the semi-wooded path that rises gently. After you cross a small stream keep right of some ruined buildings on the hillside just above. These belong to the former Fairest Clough Farm, one of several long-deserted dwellings which once existed in Bretton Clough.

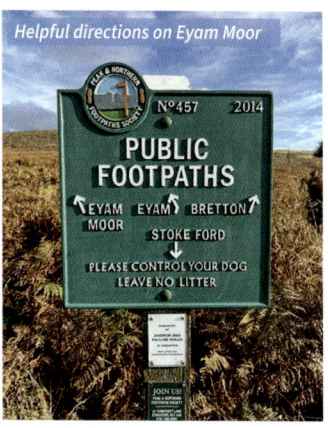

Helpful directions on Eyam Moor

Beautiful mixed woodland in Bretton Clough

WALK 12 – BRETTON CLOUGH

Continue across the open valley floor of **Bretton Clough** and stay on the path until you re-enter woodland and descend to a stile before a stream.

Because Bretton Clough is so well hidden, it's said that in 1745 farmers from Eyam drove their cattle into the valley to conceal them from Bonnie Prince Charlie's invading army, as the Highlanders marched through Derbyshire on their way south.

5 Cross the stream and climb up the path opposite. Turn sharply left at a gate and follow this steep and winding path up through woodland until you reach a junction by a bench. Turn left and continue up the path. After 50m turn right on a narrow, fenced path up across the hillside to buildings. Turn right onto the lane to return to the start. Look west and you may see giant white gliders from the Derbyshire and Lancashire Gliding Club circling gracefully in the skies.

Exposed to the elements on Eyam Edge

The Barrel Inn at Bretton is Derbyshire's highest pub (381m above sea level) and on a clear day the views from this exposed position on Eyam Edge are truly expansive. The 400-year-old building was once a farmhouse and its thick stone walls and huge fireplace are an indication that the weather up here is not always benign. A severe and prolonged snowstorm in January 1947 resulted in 6m high drifts and the pub was completely cut off for almost a fortnight. Rescuers said that the building looked like a 'huge igloo' and they had to dig where they thought the front door was located. Miraculously publican Stanley Drewett and his wife emerged alive.

The sturdily built Barrel Inn at Bretton

A tomb in Eyam churchyard

WALK 13
Eyam

Start/finish	Eyam Museum, Hawkhill Road
Locate	///otherwise.pigs.cases
Cafes/pubs	Pub and cafes in Eyam
Transport	Buses from Sheffield, Bakewell and Buxton
Parking	Car parks in Hawkhill Road, Eyam (S32 5QW)
Toilets	Near car park

Time 2hr
Distance 5.5km (3.4 miles)
Climb 180m

A short but undulating walk to learn about a village forever associated with a tale of sacrifice and hope

Eyam (pronounced 'eem') is best known for a collective act of extraordinary self-sacrifice during an outbreak of plague in 1665–66. This walk begins with a long but steady pull up field and woodland paths to the hilltop above the village, then goes on to explore many of the sites associated with the famous episode, ending at the excellent Eyam Museum, where you can learn more about the village's rich social history.

Eyam Museum, complete with a rat weathervane!

Mompesson's Well

1 From **Eyam Museum** walk down the road and turn right at the bottom. After 200m turn right up a driveway between cottages, signposted as a public footpath. At the end continue through fields, going to the left of a house and steadily uphill into woods. The path levels out and drops down to cross **Jumber Brook** on the right. At the far end of the path turn left onto a track up to the road.

2 Turn right and walk along the lane for 750m until you reach a junction. Go left for a short distance to visit **Mompesson's Well**.

Mompesson's Well is named after the local rector at the time of the plague. Located on the edge of the parish, it was where villagers left money in the water (supposedly to cleanse it) in exchange for food and other essentials supplied from outside.

3 Walk back down the lane towards Eyam and 75m past the junction go left on a public footpath. This follows the top edge of a plantation, then drops gradually down the wooded hillside to emerge at the end of Riley Back Lane in **Eyam**. Continue down to a junction.

Eyam village

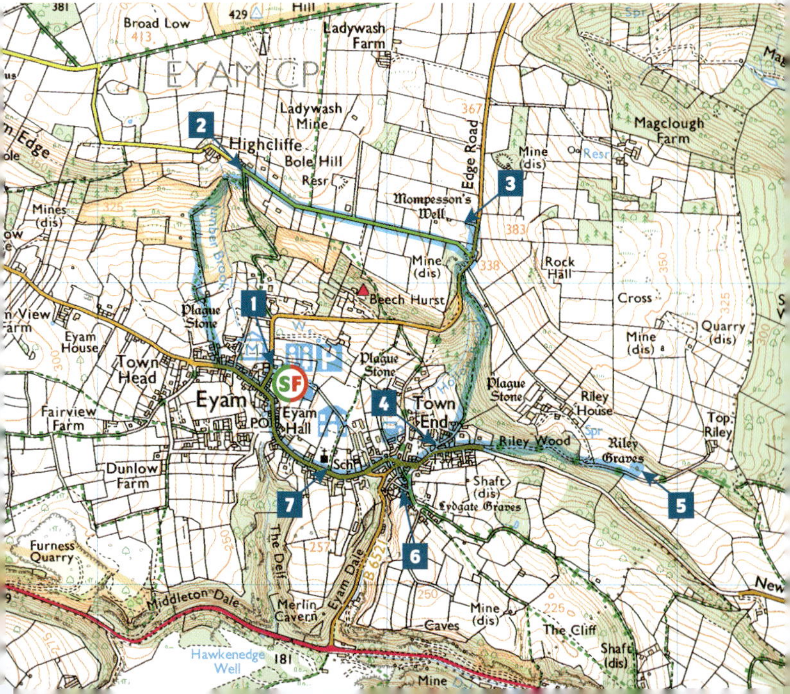

Plague Cottage, where the first victim died

4 Turn left, then left again onto Riley Lane for 500m to visit **Riley Graves** (keep right at a fork, signposted Top Riley). Riley Graves contain the six gravestones and tomb of the whole Hancock family, who perished in the outbreak of plague.

5 Retrace your steps along the lane to rejoin the road through the village until you reach The Square in the centre. Just beyond Eyam Cafe turn left and walk up Lydgate for 100m to visit **Lydgate Grave** on the right.

6 Return to The Square, cross the road and turn left to walk up Church Street to the **Parish Church of St Lawrence**.

In the south aisle of Eyam church is the so-called Plague Register, a copy of the parish register of the time that lists all the people who died in Eyam during the plague.

7 Continue along the pavement past Plague Cottage. This small terraced cottage was where George Viccars, the first plague victim, died on 7 September 1665. Beyond **Eyam Hall** turn right into Hawkhill Road to return to the start.

– To shorten

At Waypoint 4 omit the there-and-back to Riley Graves and instead continue down into the village centre, saving 1.5km (40min).

Eyam, the plague and learning from history

Riley Graves on the hillside outside Eyam

The plague arrived in Eyam in the summer of 1665 via a bundle of damp cloth from London containing infected fleas. It quickly swept through the small community and more and more people died, but instead of taking flight the whole village, led by the rector William Mompesson, quarantined itself to stop wider contagion. When it finally abated 14 months later a total of 260 residents had perished; and some of the family graves from this time can be visited on the walk. Fast forward 350 years and Eyam's story of a selfless community in lockdown in the face of a deadly disease was re-told with added poignancy during the 2020 Covid pandemic. To learn more visit Eyam Museum (www.eyam-museum.org.uk).

Upper Burbage Bridge at the start of the walk

WALK 14
Higger Tor and Carl Wark

Start/finish	*Upper Burbage Bridge*
Locate	*///ports.pop.thus*
Cafes/pubs	*None on route*
Transport	*No public transport*
Parking	*Upper Burbage Bridge car park, Ringinglow Road (S32 1BR)*
Toilets	*No public toilets on route*

Time 1hr 30min
Distance 5km (3.1 miles)
Climb 115m

An absorbing ramble around a high moorland valley via a prehistoric hillfort

This short and fairly straightforward walk explores the upper reaches of Burbage Brook through an open valley ringed by crags and heather moorland. Along the way are two prominent gritstone outcrops, including the atmospheric site of an Iron Age hillfort. There are a couple of descents that are rocky underfoot, but the mild scramble down from the top of Carl Wark can be avoided using a shortcut.

Higger Tor and Upper Burbage valley

Abandoned millstones near Higger Tor

1 Go through the gate at the car park by **Upper Burbage Bridge** and out onto the moor. The name Burbage comes from Old English and means 'stream near a fortified place'. Take the upper of two paths ahead, keeping to the high rim of the valley. Follow this all the way to the top of **Higger Tor** in sight ahead.

2 Go over to the far (southern) edge of the broad flat summit and turn right. In 150m head sharply left down a slanting path back through the rocks to the moorland below. Take the left of two paths, making directly for the flat top of Cark Wark 500m away, until you reach a path junction just before the path steepens.

Since medieval times the gritstone escarpments around Burbage were quarried to make millstones, used in the milling of cereals or for crushing lead ore. Circular and with a hole in the middle, these giant stones have since become the emblem of the Peak District National Park.

3 Go straight ahead and up the rough steps onto the summit of **Cark**

WALK 14 – HIGGER TOR AND CARL WARK

Wark. Keep left and after 150m look for a narrow path that winds its way steeply down between the rocks on your left. Follow this down the open hillside to reach an old packhorse bridge.

4 Cross over **Burbage Brook** and follow the wide track up the hillside beyond until you reach a junction.

Packhorse bridge over Burbage Brook

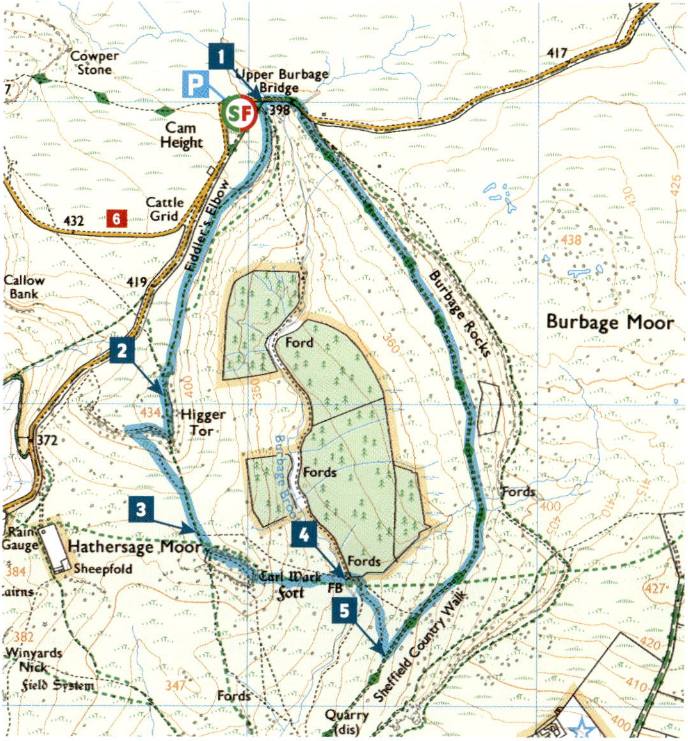

The conifers in the valley bottom are remnants of a larger plantation that dates from the late 1960s, but in recent years much of the larch and pine has been removed and the open moorland restored to provide a more natural and wildlife-friendly habitat.

5 Turn left and follow the popular track past **Burbage Rocks** for 2km until you reach the road at the head of the valley. Go through the gate and turn left to walk along the roadside to the car park, or for a more adventurous ending clamber across the rocks below the bridge and back up to the start.

Upper Burbage was used by Canadian soldiers for training ahead of the D-Day landings in June 1944, and if you look closely at the larger boulders either side of the path after Waypoint 5 you'll see some with bullet holes and mortar shell scars that date from this time.

— To shorten

To avoid the rocky scramble down from the summit of Carl Wark (and save 50m of ascent) turn left at Waypoint 3 and follow this easier path below the hillfort all the way down to the footbridge at Waypoint 4.

Carl Wark (left) and Higger Tor from Upper Burbage Bridge

WALK 14 – HIGGER TOR AND CARL WARK

Bullet marks on a boulder used as target practice

Interpreting the landscape

Ancient defences on Carl Wark

From the top of Higger Tor look down at Carl Wark and see how this long but flat rocky promontory, with sheer drops on two sides, must have provided an obvious defensive position for prehistoric tribes around 2500 years ago. They dug earthen banks around the summit plateau, some faced with stones and boulders which are still visible today. But despite plenty of studies and speculation, including an excavation in 1951, it's still unclear whether this hilltop enclosure simply provided shelter, perhaps with crude dwellings, or given the limited space and rocky ground maybe it was a place for ceremonial gatherings?

Woodland rides at Longshaw

WALK 15
Longshaw

Time 1hr 30min
Distance 4.9km (3 miles)
Climb 95m

This easy tour of the National Trust's Longshaw estate takes in moorland, woods and scenic parkland

Start/finish	*Longshaw Visitor Centre*
Locate	*///slime.crowd.event*
Cafes/pubs	*Cafe at Longshaw Visitor Centre*
Transport	*Buses from Sheffield to Fox House (400m from start)*
Parking	*National Trust Woodcroft car park, Longshaw (S11 7TZ)*
Toilets	*At Longshaw Visitor Centre*

The National Trust's Longshaw estate is part of the wider Eastern Moors that are managed by a partnership of conservation bodies. It's a mix of ancient woodland, open pasture and heather-covered moorland, as well as peaty-brown streams gurgling their way down to the valley far below. This scenic route weaves its way through all these habitats on easy paths and via modest slopes.

Longshaw Visitor Centre

Longshaw is a great place for family walks

1 From the cafe walk a few paces down to the surfaced driveway (to the Lodge) just below, with the open moorland beyond. Turn right and follow it to the end, cross the B6521 and continue down the track. Fork left, then at a junction swing left and down to cross a small footbridge.

2 Follow the path downstream beside **Burbage Brook** for 1.6km, before crossing back over via another footbridge and up to the road.

Burbage Brook now leaves the open moorland to tumble down the rocky cleft of Padley Gorge in spectacular fashion amid ancient birch and oak woodland. Many of trees are stunted and twisted and covered in moss and lichen in a very Tolkienesque manner.

One of Longshaw's tumbling streams

3 Cross the road and continue past the National Trust's Granby Discovery Barn into woodland. Follow the path as far as a large pond. The pond was originally created as a fishing lake and once had a boathouse and pier.

WALK 15 – LONGSHAW

4 On the far side of the pond turn right for a path signposted Yarncliff. Go through a gate and down the hillside until you reach a wide track. Turn left and follow this down to a junction, swinging left and uphill, initially with a stream on your left. Continue gradually uphill to reach a crossroads of tracks. Keep your eyes peeled for the large herd of wild Red deer which roam Longshaw and the adjoining moors.

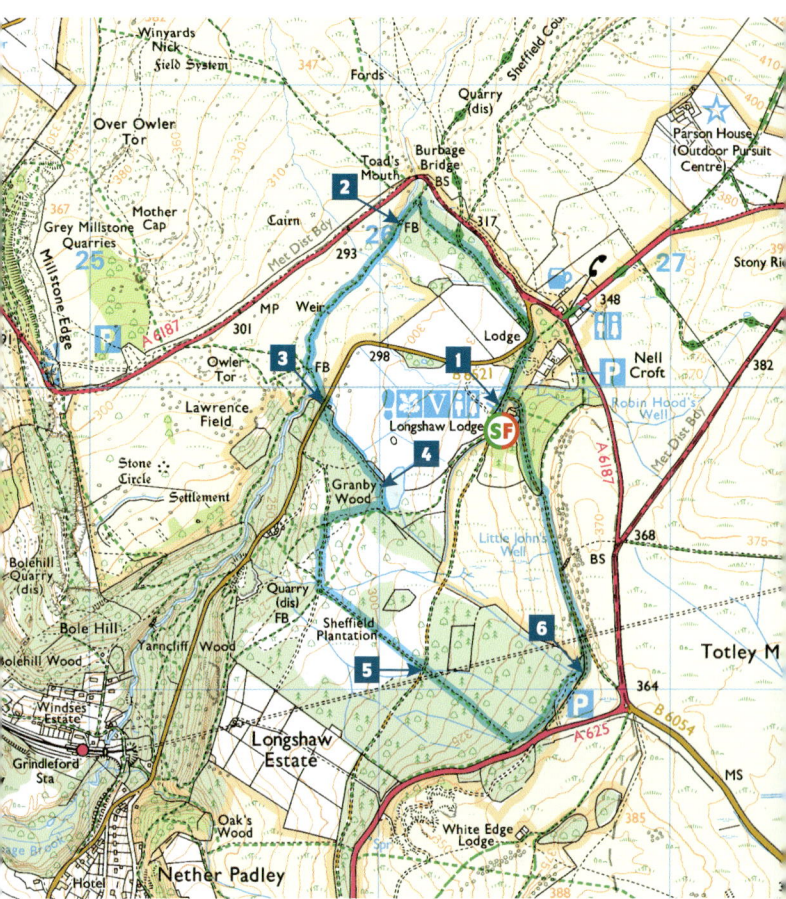

SHORT WALKS PEAK DISTRICT

5 Go straight over and maintain this direct route, which continues to climb gently through trees. At the top it swings left and reaches a small car park. Walk to the far end and go through a pedestrian gap in the wall on the right to reach a wide track above. This location is known as Wooden Pole after the nearby and historic hilltop post, possibly once a boundary marker or guidepost for early travellers.

6 Turn left and follow the level route along the upper slopes with great views over the estate. Go through a gate and continue through woods to return to the visitor centre next to **Longshaw Lodge**.

The Longshaw Sheep Dog Trials take place at the end of each summer in the meadows below Longshaw Lodge. They were first held in 1898 and claim to be the oldest continuous trials in the country.

– To shorten

At Waypoint 5 turn left at the crossroads of tracks and follow this directly back to the visitor centre, saving just under 1km (30min).

Longshaw Estate – from shooting to rambling

Longshaw once belonged to the Duke of Rutland, who used it as a shooting estate. The Lodge, next to today's visitor centre, was built in 1827 to accommodate his VIP guests, including George V and the Duke of Wellington, who came here to 'bag' grouse in large numbers. It

Longshaw Lodge

was later used as a military hospital, then a guest house, before being converted into private apartments. In 1931 the whole estate was acquired by the National Trust and today the focus is on conservation and recreation, with a well-maintained network of paths and waymarked trails.

USEFUL INFORMATION

Tourism bodies

Visit Peak District & Derbyshire
www.visitpeakdistrict.com

Peak District National Park
www.peakdistrict.gov.uk

National Trust
www.nationaltrust.org.uk

Eastern Moors
www.visit-eastern-moors.org.uk

Severn Trent Water
www.stwater.co.uk/
our-visitor-sites/
upper-derwent-valley

Tourist information centres

Castleton, Hope Valley
www.peakdistrict.gov.uk/visiting/
visitor-centres/castleton

Buses

Bus from Sheffield
www.firstbus.co.uk

Bus from Buxton
www.highpeakbuses.com

Buses from Buxton and Sheffield
www.stagecoachbus.com

Buses from Bakewell and Sheffield
www.andrews-of-tideswell.co.uk

Trains

Trains from Manchester and Sheffield
www.northernrailway.co.uk

© Andrew McCloy 2025
First edition 2025
ISBN: 978 1 78631 258 7
eISBN: 978 1 78765 226 2

Printed in Singapore by KHL Printing using responsibly sourced paper.
A catalogue record for this book is available from the British Library.
All photographs are by the author unless otherwise stated.
Cover illustration of Higger Tor by Clare Crooke.

© Crown copyright and database rights 2025 OS AC0000810376

Cicerone's EU representative for GPSR compliance is Easy Access System Europe, Mustamäe tee 50, 10621 Tallinn, Estonia. Email gpsr.requests@easproject.com.

CICERONE

Cicerone Press, Juniper House, Murley Moss, Oxenholme Road,
Kendal, Cumbria, LA9 7RL

www.cicerone.co.uk

Updates to this Guide

While every effort is made to ensure the accuracy of guidebooks as they go to print, changes can occur during the lifetime of an edition. Any updates that we know of for this guide will be on the Cicerone website (www.cicerone.co.uk/1258/updates), so please check before planning your trip. We also advise that you check information about transport, accommodation and shops locally. Even rights of way can be altered over time. We are always grateful for information about any discrepancies between a guidebook and the facts on the ground, sent by email to updates@cicerone.co.uk.

Register your book: To sign up to receive free updates, special offers and GPX files where available, create a Cicerone account and register your purchase via the 'My Account' tab at www.cicerone.co.uk.